D1190675

Mighty Machines

Snowplows

by Terri DeGezelle

Consulting Editor: Gail Saunders-Smith, PhD

Consultant: Tammy Higham, CAE
Snow and Ice Management Association
Erie, Pennsylvania

Capstone press
Mankato, Minnesota

Pebble Plus is published by Capstone Press,
151 Good Counsel Drive, P.O. Box 669, Mankato, Minnesota 56002.
www.capstonepress.com

1 2 3 4 5 6 11 10 09 08 07 06

Library of Congress Cataloging-in-Publication Data
DeGezelle, Terri, 1955–
    Snowplows / by Terri DeGezelle.
    p. cm.—(Pebble plus. Mighty machines)
    Summary: "Simple text and photographs present snowplows, their parts, and their jobs"—Provided by
publisher.
    Includes bibliographical references and index.
    ISBN-13: 978-0-7368-5357-6 (hardcover)
    ISBN-10: 0-7368-5357-X (hardcover)
    1. Snowplows—Juvenile literature. 2. Snow removal—Juvenile literature. I. Title. II. Series.
TD868.D44 2006
629.225—dc22   2005021606

Editorial Credits
Martha E. H. Rustad, editor; Molly Nei, set designer; Ted Williams, book designer;
    Wanda Winch, photo researcher; Scott Thoms, photo editor

Photo Credits
Capstone Press/Karon Dubke, cover; Corbis/Reuters, 7; Digital Vision Ltd., 1; The Image Works/Chet
Gordon, 13; The Image Works/David M. Jennings, 17; The Image Works/Syracuse Newspapers/John Berry, 11;
iStockphoto Inc./Benoit Beauregar, 21; Peter Arnold, Inc./Craig Newbauer, 19; Photri-MicroStock/M. Boroff, 15;
SuperStock/age fotostock, 9; Wolfgang Kaehler, 5

The author thanks Jerry O'Meara, Heavy Equipment Operator, City of Mankato, Minnesota, for his assistance
with this book. Pebble Plus thanks Jerry Strobel, Street Maintenance, City of Glencoe, Minnesota, for his
assistance with this book. Pebble Plus also thanks the Hennepin County Highway Department for assistance
with photo shoots.

Note to Parents and Teachers

The Mighty Machines set supports national standards related to science, technology, and
society. This book describes and illustrates snowplows. The images support early readers
in understanding the text. The repetition of words and phrases helps early readers learn
new words. This book also introduces early readers to subject-specific vocabulary words,
which are defined in the Glossary section. Early readers may need assistance to read
some words and to use the Table of Contents, Glossary, Read More, Internet Sites, and
Index sections of the book.

Table of Contents

A Snowplow's Job

Snowplows clear snow away
after snowstorms.
Snowplows make snowy roads
safe for travel.

Snowplows push snow off
airport runways.
They clear parking lots
and driveways.

Parts of Snowplows

Snowplow blades

scrape up snow.

They push the snow

to the side of the road.

Snowplow drivers sit
in the cab.
They use levers to move
the blade.

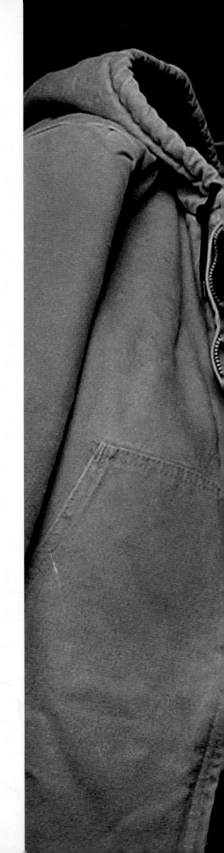

Snowplows have
flashing lights.
The lights warn people
to be careful
around snowplows.

Big snowblowers
work on highways.
They have turning blades
that blow snow off roads.

blade

15

What Snowplows Do

Groups of snowplows
work together
to clear big roads quickly.

Snowplows clear the way
for spreader trucks.
Spreader trucks drop sand
or salt on roads.
Sand and salt make
icy roads safer for travel.

Mighty Snowplows

Snowplows make winter roads
safe for cars and trucks.
Snowplows are
mighty machines.

Glossary

blade—a sharp piece of metal on a snowplow that pushes snow; blades on snowblowers turn to blow snow off roads.

cab—an enclosed area of a truck or other vehicle where the driver sits

flashing—turning on and off

lever—a bar or handle used to control a machine

runway—a long, flat strip of ground where airplanes take off and land

warn—to tell people about danger

Read More

Bridges, Sarah. *I Drive a Snowplow.* Working Wheels. Minneapolis: Picture Window Books, 2005.

Randolph, Joanne. *Snowplows.* Road Machines. New York: PowerKids Press, 2002.

Internet Sites

FactHound offers a safe, fun way to find Internet sites related to this book. All of the sites on FactHound have been researched by our staff.

Here's how:

1. Visit *www.facthound.com*

2. Type in this special code **073685357X** for age-appropriate sites. Or enter a search word related to this book for a more general search.

3. Click on the **Fetch It** button.

FactHound will fetch the best sites for you!

Index

Word Count: 127
Grade: 1
Early-Intervention Level: 14